inspirations

STAINED GLASS

Over 20 beautiful projects for the home

inspirations

STAINED GLASS

Over 20 beautiful projects for the home

DEIRDRE O'MALLEY

PHOTOGRAPHY BY LIZZIE ORME

LORENZ BOOKS

This edition published in 1998 by Lorenz Books

© Anness Publishing Limited 1998

Lorenz Books is an imprint of
Anness Publishing Limited
Hermes House
88–89 Blackfriars Road
London SE1 8HA

This edition distributed in Canada by Raincoast Books
8680 Cambie Street
Vancouver
British Columbia V6P 6M9

ISBN 1 85967 654 5
A CIP catalogue record for this book is available from the British Library

Publisher: Joanna Lorenz
Project Editor: Cathy Marriott
Designer: Ian Sandom
Photographer: Lizzie Orme
Stylist: Katie Gibbs
Illustrators: Madeleine David and Lucinda Ganderton

Printed in Hong Kong

1 3 5 7 9 10 8 6 4 2

Please note: When working with glass, whenever possible always wear a pair of safety goggles to protect your eyes from
glass shards and wear a pair of rubber gloves or barrier cream to protect your hands from toxic lead.

CONTENTS

INTRODUCTION

One of the most pleasing things about walking into the interior of an old church, particularly during the summer, is looking up at the rich, translucent colours of the stained glass windows. The intensity of the colours of stained glass is a really beautiful sight and the way the light is diffused by the glass has always fascinated me and made me wish that I could recreate the look of stained glass at home.

This book is designed to inspire you to make the most of stained glass so you can add unique decorative touches to your home. We are not suggesting that you make your own enormous church windows but we do have a range of projects for you to create the effect of stained glass where you choose. There are projects as small and simple as painted salt and pepper pots and easy-to-make window hangings to indoor glass lanterns and larger, more elaborate glass door panels.

This book features clear step-by-step photography to guide you through basic stained glass techniques, then moves on to larger projects for more experienced craft artists. Templates for the projects are included, together with information on materials required. Designs range from paint effects that cleverly give the illusion of stained glass to making pieces using glass nuggets in gorgeous colours. To create the genuine article, there are projects to make cabinet door panels that use lead came and cut-out pieces of stained glass.

Whether you choose to make just one simple project, or give all of your cupboard doors a lavish and authentic stained glass panel, your home will be enriched by the effect of the glorious colours that only stained glass can bring.

Deborah Barker

BANDED VASE

By filling the vase with water first, you can ensure that the lines of your decorative border will be accurate. The stained glass effect is created with glass paints and the stick-on lead is added afterwards.

YOU WILL NEED

square vase
water-based marker pen
ruler
black contour paste
sponge scourer
craft knife and cutting mat
glass paints in yellow, orange, red, violet
colourless medium
spatula
3 mm/⅛ in self-adhesive lead
scissors
fid

1 Depending on the proportions of the vase, gauge by eye the position of the borders. Using a water-based marker pen, draw the position of the lower border. Pour water into the vase up to this point. Stand the vase on a level surface and draw around the vase at the water level. Mark the position of the top border. Top up the water to this level and draw the second line around the vase.

2 Mark the simple pattern on to the surface of the vase with the marker pen and a ruler.

3 Go over the lines with black contour paste and leave to dry.

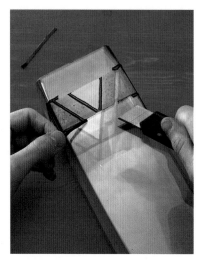

4 Cut sponge scourer into pieces to match the shapes of the design. Mix each paint colour with an equal amount of colourless medium and sponge the paint over the vase using a different piece of sponge for each colour. Leave to dry for 24 hours.

5 Put the vase on to the cutting mat. Using a craft knife, score around the edge of each cell. Use the very tip of the craft knife to lift up the contour paste and carefully peel it off the vase.

6 Cut pieces of self-adhesive lead slightly oversize for all of the shorter lines. Peel off the backing paper and press them in place. Trim the ends of each piece at an angle with a craft knife.

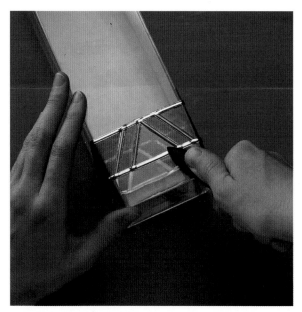

7 Cut two strips of lead for the two border lines and press them into place.

8 Rub over all the lead lines with a fid to press them firmly in place.

MOSAIC LANTERN

The nightlight concealed inside illuminates this glass lantern at night to bring out the richness of the colours. The lantern is made by using a plain drinking glass as the base and adding a mosaic of tiny glass squares.

YOU WILL NEED
indelible black pen
metal straight-edge
pieces of stained glass in blue, green, red
and yellow
glass cutter
heavy-based glass tumbler
ultra-violet glue
spatula and bowl
tile grout
black acrylic paint
sponge scourer
nightlight

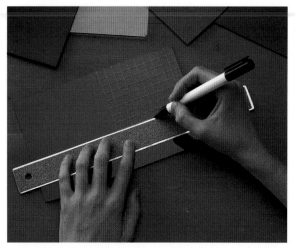

1 Using an indelible black pen and a metal straight-edge, mark a grid of 1 cm/⅜ in squares on a piece of stained glass.

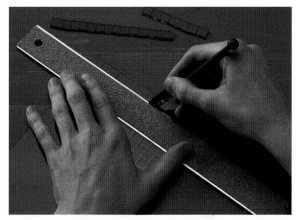

2 Cut the glass into 1 cm/⅜ in lengths by scoring the glass with a glass cutter, using the straight-edge as a guide. Tap the underside of the score line with the hammer end of the glass cutter, then snap the glass apart between both thumbs.

3 Score the glass strip into 1 cm/⅜ in squares. Turn the strip over so the score lines face the worktop and tap each score line with the hammer end of the glass cutter. The glass should break easily into squares.

4 Using ultra-violet glue, stick the glass mosaic pieces around the glass, working from top to bottom. Leave a gap of 2 mm /¹⁄₁₆ in between squares to allow for grouting.

5 In a bowl, mix 30 ml/2 tbsp of tile grout with 25 ml/1½ tbsp of cold water and a 5 cm/2 in length of black acrylic paint. Stir until it forms a smooth, dark grey paste.

6 Using a spatula, press the grout mixture into the gaps between the mosaic pieces. Remove excess grout with the spatula, then allow to dry.

7 When the grout is dry, use a damp sponge scourer to clean any remaining smears of grout from the surface of the mosaic pieces.

8 When the lantern is clean, place a nightlight inside. Never leave burning candles unattended and always keep them out of the reach of children.

CURTAIN DECORATIONS

These stained glass pendants will shimmer in the diffused light from the window. Add decorative motifs cut from acetate and hang on gauzy material so as to allow the light and colours to really shine through.

YOU WILL NEED
copyright-free pictures of shells (see templates)
photocopier
acetate sheets
small, sharp scissors
pieces of stained glass
glass cutter
4 mm/³⁄₁₆ in copper foil
fid
solder and soldering iron
flux
epoxy glue
copper wire
small pliers
hooks and eyes
white sewing thread
sewing needle
white muslin curtain

1 Photocopy pictures of different shaped shells on to acetate sheets. Cut out the shells very close to the edge of the image.

2 Draw stencils of a triangle and a square, a large and a small one of each. Cut out glass shapes in several colours, using the stencils as a guide.

3 Wrap copper foil around the edges of the bigger pieces of glass.

4 Use a fid to flatten the edges of the copper foil around the pieces of glass.

5 Solder over the copper foil to make it silver. The heat will make the copper turn a silver colour.

6 Take a soldered piece of glass and a smaller piece of the same shape. Place a small blob of glue on each piece of glass, then put the photocopied image on to the big piece and place the smaller piece over the top. Press to make the glue spread.

7 Using a pair of small pliers, bend the copper wire into small hooks. Make a hook for each decoration you have made.

8 Solder the hook to the copper foil, remembering to flux the wire and the soldered edge.

9 Sew the eyes from several hooks and eyes to the top edge of the curtain and hook on the curtain decorations. Fold the curtain over a pole so that the decorations are hanging in the top third of the window.

LEADED PICTURE FRAMES

Give pictures a touch of grandeur with this richly coloured frame made from glass paints and stick-on lead. Choose the paint colours to complement the colours in the picture you have chosen to frame.

YOU WILL NEED
clip frame (glass/backing board/clips)
paper and pencil
metal straight-edge
ruler
indelible black pen
3 mm/⅛ in self-adhesive lead
craft knife and cutting mat
boning peg
glass paints
paintbrush
turpentine

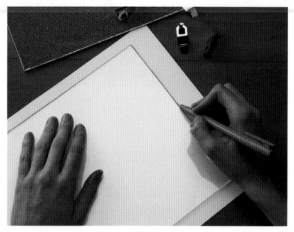

1 Remove clips and backing board from the clip frame. Place the glass on some paper and draw around it to create a template.

2 Using a pencil and ruler, draw a simple linear design within the template.

3 Place the glass over the template and trace the design on to the glass using an indelible black pen.

4 Stretch the lead by pulling it gently. Cut four lengths to fit around the outside edge of the frame, using a sharp craft knife. Remove backing paper from the lead and stick in place.

5 Measure the lead needed for the inner framework and cut with a craft knife by using a side-to-side rocking motion. Hold the knife blade at a 90° angle to the lead to ensure a straight cut.

6 With the edges butted closely together, peel away the backing paper from the lead strips and press gently into place with your fingertips or a boning peg.

7 Once in the correct position, press firmly along the length of the lead using a boning peg to seal it to the glass.

8 With the pointed end of the boning peg, press around the outer edges of each strip of lead to neaten the edges and prevent the glass paints from running.

9 Colour in the design using glass paints, cleaning the paintbrush with turpentine between colours. Leave to dry. Replace backing board, add a picture of your choice and clip into place.

DIAMOND-PATTERNED CARAFE

Lines of etched and coloured glass bring this carafe to life. Strips of masking tape quickly screen off the areas of the carafe ready for painting with etching paste. Fill the decorated carafe with homemade lemonade and plenty of ice.

YOU WILL NEED
glass carafe
masking tape
small, sharp scissors
rubber gloves
etching paste
paintbrush
clean cotton rag
pieces of stained glass
glass cutter
pliers
epoxy glue

1 Mask off (wrap) the carafe with masking tape to make rings around the carafe.

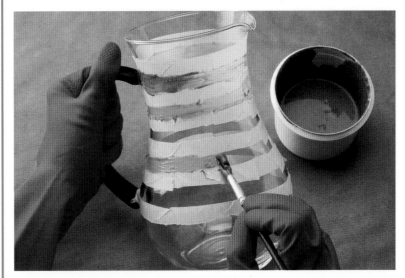

2 Wearing rubber gloves, paint the etching paste on to the exposed glass. Leave for 3 minutes.

21

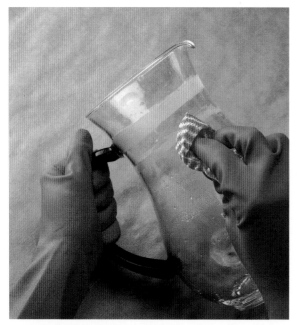

3 Wash off the paste and remove the masking tape. Wipe the carafe dry.

4 Using a glass cutter and pliers, cut out small glass squares and triangles to fit around the carafe.

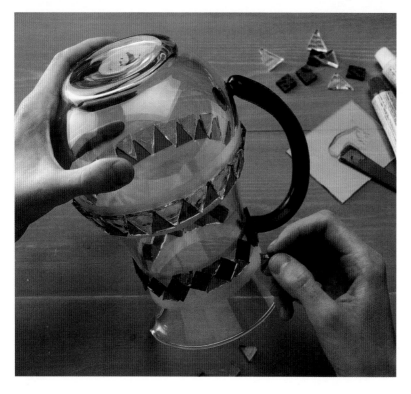

5 Glue several pieces at a time and leave the glue to dry a little so that the pieces do not slide about. Once you have finished one row, fit the other pieces in between the first ones. For the bottom row of the top section, turn the carafe upside down to steady the pieces as you glue them on.

FRINGED CANDLESTICK

The fringe of coloured glass strips on this candlestick will catch the light and tinkle in the slightest breeze. Add as few or as many glass strips as you like and space evenly around the rim for an original and attractive table centrepiece.

YOU WILL NEED
pen and ruler
pieces of stained glass
glass cutter
straight-edge
pliers, square-nosed and long-nosed
copper foil, 6 mm/¼ in and 4 mm/³⁄₁₆ in wide
fid
solder
soldering iron
bulldog clip
tumbler
jump rings, 5 mm/⅛ in and 6 mm/¼ in
candlestick with a rim

1 With the pen and ruler, draw out 6 mm/¼ in wide strips on to the stained glass.

2 Score a few lines at a time using a glass cutter and straight-edge. Tap along the first scored line with the ball of the glass cutter on the reverse of the glass.

3 With the square-nosed pliers, loosen the scored line and break off the glass. Repeat the process until you have as many strips as you want.

4 Edge each glass strip with the 4 mm/³⁄₁₆ in copper foil; keep the edges as straight as possible.

5 Press down the copper foil with a fid.

6 Solder each piece of foiled glass. The copper will turn a silver colour.

7 Using a bulldog clip and a tumbler, prop the clip into a secure position. Place the strips of glass, one piece at a time, into the clip using long-nosed pliers. Position one of the larger jump rings in the top centre of the glass strip at a right angle to the glass.

8 Build up a couple of layers of 6 mm/¼ in copper foil around the rim of the candlestick.

9 Press down on the copper foil to firmly position it and solder it all the way round.

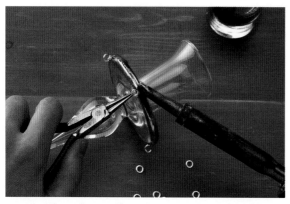

10 Place the candlestick on its side and start to solder the larger jump rings around the edge at regular intervals.

11 Attach strips of glass to the rim using smaller jump rings so they hang level.

LEADED DOOR PANELS

The etched glass panels on this old door have been painted with glass paints and finished with stick-on lead. The finished effect has a much lighter look than genuine stained glass made with lead came.

YOU WILL NEED

door with two sandblasted glass panels
tape measure
paper and pencil
ruler
felt-tipped pen
scissors
masking tape
indelible black pen
self-adhesive lead 1 cm/⅜ in wide
craft knife and cutting mat
boning peg
glass paints in turquoise, green, yellow and light green
turpentine
small paintbrushes

1 Measure the glass panels with a tape measure. With a pencil, draw panels to scale on a piece of paper. Using a ruler, draw your design within the panel area, including 1 cm/⅜ in wide dividing lines to allow for the leading. Trace over the finished design in felt-tipped pen, cross hatching the lead lines.

2 Cut out this paper pattern with scissors and stick it to the reverse of the glass panel with lengths of masking tape.

3 Trace the design from the paper pattern on to the sandblasted side of the glass using an indelible black pen. When the tracing is complete, remove the paper pattern.

4 Stretch the lead by gently pulling it. Cut four lengths to fit around the edge of the glass panel, using a sharp craft knife. Remove the backing paper and stick the lead in place.

5 Measure the lead needed for the inner framework and cut with a knife using a side-to-side rocking motion. Keep the blade at a 90° angle to the lead to ensure a straight cut. Cut and stick longer lengths of lead first, then work the smaller pieces.

6 With the edges butted closely together, remove the backing paper from the lead and press into place with your fingertips. Then press firmly along the length of the lead with a boning peg to seal it to the glass. Press around the outer edges of the lead with the pointed end of the boning peg to achieve a neat watertight finish.

7 Dilute the glass paints with 30% turpentine to create a subtle, watercolour feel to the paint. Use a small paintbrush to colour in the small areas between the leading. Clean brushes with turpentine between colours.

8 Once the intricate areas are coloured in, paint the remainder of the design, leaving the centre of the glass panel unpainted or painting the whole area if you prefer. Leave to dry.

SUN LIGHT CATCHER

Stained glass is made for sunlight, and this sun light catcher can hang in any window in the house to catch all of the available light. Gold outlining paste separates the coloured areas and adds an extra special shine.

YOU WILL NEED
20 cm/8 in diameter clear glass roundel,
4 mm/³⁄₁₆ in thick
paper and pencil
indelible black pen
gold outlining paste
glass paints in orange, yellow, red and
blue
small paintbrushes
turpentine
73 cm/29 in length of chain
pliers
epoxy glue

1 Make a template by drawing round the rim of the glass roundel.

2 Trace the sun motif template from the back of the book, enlarging to the size required.

3 Place the circle of glass over the template and trace the design on to the glass using an indelible black pen.

4 Trace over the black lines using gold outlining paste. Leave to dry.

5 Colour in the central sun motif using orange and yellow glass paints. Leave to dry. Clean brushes with turpentine.

6 Fill in the rest of the design using red and blue glass paints. Leave to dry.

7 Place chain around the edge of the glass and cut to size. Rejoin the links by squeezing firmly together with pliers.

8 Cut an 8 cm/3¼ in length of chain, open the links at each end, and attach it to the chain circle by squeezing with pliers. Glue the chain around the circumference of the glass using epoxy glue.

DOOR NUMBER PLAQUE

Create your own personalized number plate to make your house stand out from the rest.
Glass nuggets come in a wide range of colours and you can add bright spots of colour
in the crazy patchwork of glass.

YOU WILL NEED
circle cutter
cutting oil
30 cm/12 in square of 3 mm/⅛ in clear
glass
piece of carpet or blanket
glass cutter
indelible black pen
pieces of stained glass
scythe stone
glass nuggets
ultra-violet glue
lead came
lead knife
bradawl
1.5 mm/1/16 in copper wire
round-nosed pliers
flux brush
flux
solder
soldering iron
tiling grout
black acrylic paint
spatula
plastic grout applicator
clean cotton rag

1 Set a circle cutter to cut a 20 cm/8 in diameter circle. Dip the cutter in cutting oil, position the cutter in the centre of the clear glass square and score the circle in one sweep.

2 Turn the glass over and lay it on a piece of carpet or blanket on a work surface. Press down with both thumbs just inside the scoreline until the line begins to break. Repeat until the scoreline is broken all the way around.

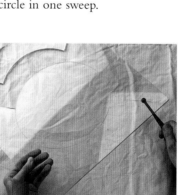

3 Score a line in from each corner of the square, stopping just before you reach the circle. With the ball of the glass cutter, tap behind each line until it cracks up to the circle. The side sections will fall away releasing the circle.

4 Trace the templates from the back of the book, enlarging to the size required. Draw around the circle of glass and write your own door number centrally within the circle using the template as a guide.

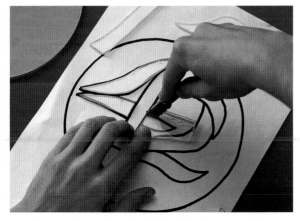

5 Score pieces of stained glass for the numerals. Break the glass by tapping behind the scoreline with the ball of the glass cutter. Remove any rough edges with a scythe stone.

6 Position several stained glass nuggets around the numerals and cut pieces of glass in contrasting colours to fill the remaining space.

7 Find a working area out of any direct sunlight (glass glue sets when it is exposed to ultra-violet light or sunlight). Apply glue to the back of each piece of glass and press it firmly into place. When all of the pieces are glued down, check their position and slide them into place if necessary.

8 Cut a length of lead came approximately 70 cm/27 in long. Use a bradawl or drill to make a small hole in the centre of the strip of came.

9 Cut a 10 cm/4 in length of copper wire. With a pair of round-nosed pliers, bend a hanging loop. Thread the ends through the hole in the came and bend them up to lock the loop in place.

▶

10 Wrap the came around the glass with the hanging loop at the top. Trim off any excess lead came with a lead knife. Flux the joint and lightly solder the ends together.

11 Mix some black acrylic paint with tiling grout. Spread it over the surface, working the mixture into the spaces between each piece of glass. Use a clean cotton rag to remove any excess. Leave to dry overnight, then polish with a clean cotton rag.

GLASS NUGGET BOTTLE HOLDER

Different-sized glass nuggets are gradually built up to create a colourful wall around the mirrored base of this bottle holder. Choose two or three shades of glass nuggets or a whole rainbow of beautiful colours, as here.

YOU WILL NEED
cutting mat
pair of compasses
indelible black pen
mirror glass
bottle
glass cutter
square-nosed pliers
copper foil, 12 mm/½ in and 4 mm/³⁄₁₆ in
fid
soldering iron and solder
flux
glass nuggets

1 On a cutting mat use a pair of compasses to draw a circle about 2.5-4 cm/ 1-1½ in larger than the base of the bottle.

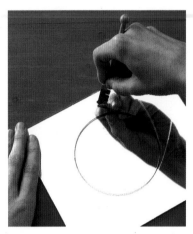

2 Score around the circle with a glass cutter. Draw lines from the edge of the circle to the edge of the mirror.

3 Tap on the reverse of the mirror with the ball of the glass cutter.

4 Loosen and break off the excess mirror with square-nosed pliers.

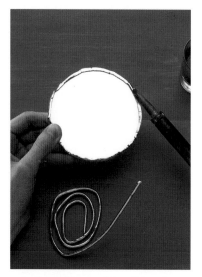

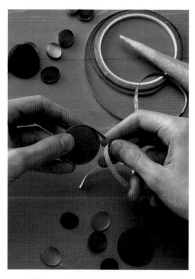

5 Wrap the 12 mm/½ in copper foil around the edge of the glass circle.

6 Press down with a fid and solder using flux and the soldering iron.

7 Select glass nuggets and wrap each one with the 4 mm/³⁄₁₆ in copper foil.

8 Solder the nuggets and start to build up an edge around the glass circle.

9 When the border is the required height, tidy up the inside and outside with the soldering iron to smooth out any drips of solder.

ETCHED BATHROOM MIRROR

Mirror tiles make inexpensive canvases for practising your stained glass techniques. This one is decorated using etching paste and coloured stained glass cut into petals and randomly arranged into pretty flowers.

YOU WILL NEED
mirror tile
felt-tipped pen
ruler
glass cutter
rubber gloves
etching paste
paintbrush
clean cotton rag
4 mm/³⁄₁₆ in copper foil
fid
flux
soldering iron and solder
brass wire
pieces of stained glass
epoxy glue

1 Mark up the size of your mirror using a felt-tipped pen on the surface of the mirror tile.

2 Cut out the mirror with a glass cutter.

3 Wearing rubber gloves and using the etching paste, paint ten or eleven four-petalled flowers around the edges of the mirror.

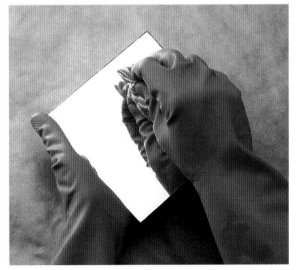

4 Wash off the etching paste after 3 minutes, and wipe the glass clean.

5 Wrap copper foil around the edge of the mirror and press down with a fid.

6 Solder around the copper foil. The heat will turn the copper foil a silver colour.

7 Cut a length of hanging wire and solder it to the edge of the mirror on each side.

8 Cut out small petal shapes in different coloured glass and stick them in flower shapes randomly around the edges of the mirror. Let the glue dry hard, and then clean the mirror with a clean cotton rag.

TRINKET BOX

A delicate little box ideal for storing necklaces, earrings or cufflinks, or to use just as a beautiful ornament. Opal glass is available from stained glass specialists and adds an extra-special lustre to your projects.

YOU WILL NEED
carbon paper
pencil
cutting square or straight-edge
glass cutter
cutting oil
blue opal glass
clear 2 mm/$\frac{1}{16}$ in picture glass
mirrored blue stained glass
copper foil, 4 mm/$\frac{3}{16}$ in and 6 mm/$\frac{1}{4}$ in
fid
safety flux
flux brush
soldering iron
50/50 tin lead solder
tinned copper wire
wire cutters
indelible black pen
scythe stone
round-nosed pliers

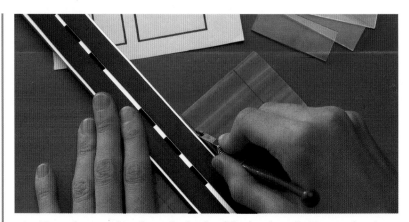

1 Trace the template from the back of the book, enlarging to the size required. Transfer the shapes to the glass using carbon paper. Using a cutting square or a thick straight-edge, score and break the side pieces of the box from clear glass and blue glass. Transfer the octagonal base outline on to the mirrored blue glass using carbon paper. Score and break the glass.

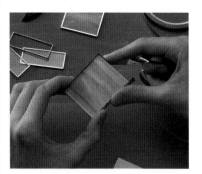

2 Wrap the blue side pieces in 6 mm/$\frac{1}{4}$ in copper foil and the thinner clear picture glass in 4 mm/$\frac{3}{16}$ in foil. Press the foil down firmly using a fid.

3 Apply lines of 4 mm/$\frac{3}{16}$ in copper foil along the edges of the top surface of the mirror base. This will ensure that the sides bond firmly to the base. Wrap the sides using 6 mm/$\frac{1}{4}$ in copper foil. Press down firmly with a fid.

4 Brush all of the copper-wrapped pieces with safety flux and lightly tack solder the pieces into place, adjusting them slightly if necessary.

5 Reflux and solder all copper surfaces. For a neat finish, run a bead of solder to fill the point where the side sections meet. Wash thoroughly to remove any traces of flux.

6 With the box balanced on one side, hold the end of a piece of wire just overlapping one of the clear glass sections. Brush with flux and touch the tip of the iron to the wire to solder it. Trim off the other end with wire cutters and repeat, applying two vertical wires for each clear glass panel.

7 Solder two horizontal pieces of wire to each pair of verticals. Solder them on oversize, then trim them to length when they are soldered in place. Wash thoroughly to remove any traces of flux. Repeat steps 6 and 7 for each clear glass pane.

8 Choose some glass for the lid and place it with the side you want to be uppermost facing down. Place the box upside down over the glass and trace around the box with an indelible black pen. Score and break the glass just inside the lines. Remove any sharp edges with a scythe stone lubricated with a little water. Wrap the edges of the lid with 6 mm/¼ in foil. Apply flux and plate the foil with solder.

9 Cut a piece of wire about 10 cm/4 in long. Using the template as a guide, bend two kinks in the wire with a pair of round-nosed pliers. Cut another 10 cm/4 in length of wire and bend two right angles in the wire to coincide with the kinks in the first wire. Bend the two ends into loops and trim off the excess wire with wire cutters.

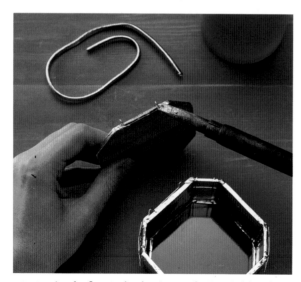

10 Apply flux to both pieces of wire. Solder the kinked section to the box and the looped section to the lid. Wash thoroughly to remove any traces of flux. Slot the lid hinge section into the body section to complete the box.

OPAL GLASS PLANTER

Planters and terrariums are ideal subjects for stained glass. The fresh white and green opal glass neatly hides the flowerpot inside. Make sure that all the joints are well soldered, otherwise your planter will not be watertight.

YOU WILL NEED
white opal glass
glass cutter
cutting square or straight-edge
round-nosed pliers
green opal glass
carbon paper
ball-point pen
scythe stone
6 mm /¼ in copper foil
fid
soldering iron
safety flux
flux brush
50/50 tin lead solder

1 Trace the template from the back of the book, enlarging to the size required. Lay the white glass over the template and score five identical pieces for the sides, using a cutting square to ensure straight lines. Use a pair of round-nosed pliers to break the glass along the scorelines. Cut strips of green glass for the bottom of each panel.

2 Lay a piece of carbon paper over the green glass and lay the template on top of the carbon paper. Transfer the shape for the top sections using a ball-point pen. Score the straight lines using the cutting square or straight-edge as a guide. Score the curved top edges and break them by tapping the underside of the glass with the ball on the end of the glass cutter. Transfer the design for the pentagonal base piece, again using carbon paper, and cut out the shape. Remove any sharp edges from the glass with a scythe stone.

3 Wrap 6 mm/¼ in copper foil around the edge of each piece and use a fid to press the foil firmly into place.

4 Allow the soldering iron to heat up. Brush on safety flux and tack solder together the three sections that make up each side panel (apply just two spots of solder along each edge).

5 Lightly tack solder one of the side panels to the base, using a minimum of solder. Position the next panel, and repeat. Tack the two panels together. Continue until all pieces are in place.

6 Reflux and solder all of the joints. Wash the planter thoroughly with hot water and washing-up liquid.

MOSAIC-BANDED CANDLE HOLDER

Bands of painted glass and stained glass mosaic turn an ordinary drinking glass into an original and attractive candle holder. Apply the paint with a small piece of sponge to give a beautifully soft, mottled effect.

YOU WILL NEED
2 brass vase caps
epoxy glue
copper wire
wire cutters
tall, straight drinking glass
masking tape
blue glass paint
sponge
turpentine
felt-tipped pen
pieces of stained glass
glass cutter

1 To make the inner piece of the candle holder, take the two vase caps and glue them together small end to small end with epoxy glue.

2 When dry, wrap the copper wire around the centre of the brass candle stand and the length of the inside of the glass to hook over the top of the glass.

3 Stick three rings of masking tape around the glass at regular intervals.

▶

4 Sponge the paint on to the glass and leave to dry. Clean the sponge with turpentine immediately afterwards or it will go hard. Remove the masking tape.

5 Using a black felt-tipped pen, draw lines on the coloured glass, 5 mm/¼ in apart. Then draw more lines at right angles to divide the glass into 5 mm/¼ in squares. Using a glass cutter, score along the lines, then break by tapping the reverse side with the hammer end of the cutter.

6 Starting with the lowest clear ring, begin sticking the squares on to the glass with epoxy glue. Use dense colours at the bottom and lighter colours further up. Stick them on a few at a time, and make sure they stick firmly and neatly.

7 Place the candle holder inside the glass lantern and hook the wire over the top of the glass. Finish the end by turning it into a spiral design.

GLASS NUGGET WALL CLOCK

An ultra-modern clock created out of plain glass and coloured glass nuggets. The edge of the circle is etched for added interest, and the clock mechanism is hidden by a circle of self-adhesive vinyl.

YOU WILL NEED
pair of compasses
self-adhesive vinyl
small, sharp scissors
glass circle, 10 cm/4 in diameter,
4 mm/³/₁₆ in thick, with a 10 mm/³/₈ in hole
cut in the centre (a glazier can do this)
etching paste
paintbrush
rubber gloves
clean cotton rag
washing-up liquid
glass nuggets, 12 large and 12 small
epoxy glue
clock mechanism for a 10 mm/³/₈ in fitting

1 Using a pair of compasses, draw two 20 cm/8 in diameter circles on to the vinyl.

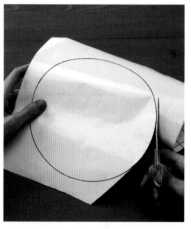

2 Cut out the circles as accurately as possible with a pair of small, sharp scissors.

3 Peel off the backing from one plastic circle and place it self-adhesive side up on the work surface. Hold the glass circle over it until there is an even border all round. Lower the glass on to the plastic and rub flat to remove any air bubbles.

4 With the plastic circle facing up, apply etching paste, with a brush, thickly and evenly, to the outer rim. Wear rubber gloves to protect your hands.

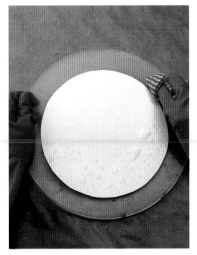

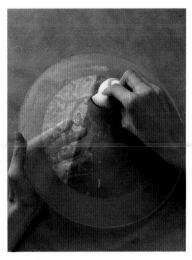

5 Leave the etching paste for 3 minutes, then wash off and dry.

6 Carefully peel off the plastic circle in the centre.

7 Clean the centre of the glass with washing-up liquid.

8 Using epoxy glue, stick each small nugget on top of a large nugget for the hours on the clock face. Leave to dry.

9 Remove the backing from the second plastic circle and place it sticky side up on the table. Hold the glass circle, etched side up, over the plastic circle and lower into position. Press flat to remove any air bubbles.

▶

10 Glue the nuggets on to the etched side to represent the 12 hours.

11 Assemble the clock mechanism by pushing the spindle through from the back, then add the central screw and the hands.

KITCHEN STORAGE JAR

Create a decorated storage jar for holding rice, pulses or dried fruit. The frosted-look background is etched first and then the flowers are painted in afterwards using a selection of brightly coloured glass paints.

YOU WILL NEED
self-adhesive vinyl
felt-tipped pen
small, sharp scissors
glass storage jar
etching paste
medium paintbrushes
rubber gloves
clean cotton rag
glass paints in various colours
clear varnish

1 Decide on an overall pattern and draw your design on to plastic with a felt-tipped pen.

2 Cut out the shapes carefully using small, sharp scissors.

3 Position the shapes on to the jar and lid in an even design and press down firmly.

59

4 Wearing rubber gloves, brush a thick and even layer of etching paste over the jar and lid. Leave to dry completely.

5 Wash the jar and lid and wipe dry using a clean cotton rag.

6 Peel off the plastic shapes. If the shapes are not deeply etched enough, then repeat the process.

7 Clean off the sticky remains of the plastic with washing-up liquid and a clean cotton rag. Paint in the shapes with coloured glass paints.

8 Leave to dry, then varnish the painted areas only with the clear varnish. When the jar is completely dry, fill as desired.

PAINTED SALT & PEPPER POTS

Create a conversation piece at mealtimes with matching salt and pepper pots. Look in kitchenware and charity shops for plain glass items to decorate, and add as much or as little decoration as you like.

YOU WILL NEED
glass salt and pepper pots
contour relief paint in black and gold
glass paints in various colours
medium paintbrushes
clear varnish

1 Draw a few loose circles on to the pots with black outline relief paint.

2 When the lines are dry, colour in the background with glass paint.

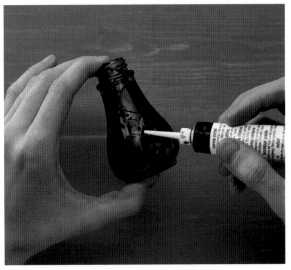

3 Fill in the circles with a different coloured paint or a variety of different colours.

4 Apply dots of black contour paint over the background colour to add texture.

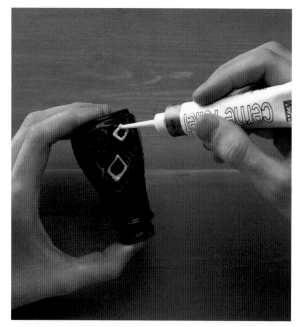

5 When dry, paint squares over the circles using the gold relief contour pen.

6 Leave the pots to dry for at least 4 hours, then paint with clear varnish.

KITCHEN CABINET DOOR PANEL

For the more experienced and confident stained glass worker, here is a stained glass cabinet door panel to make using lead came and stained glass cut to fit. Keep your early designs as simple as possible to avoid frustration and disappointment.

YOU WILL NEED
felt-tipped pen
sheets of stained glass
glass cutter
grozing pliers
masking tape
wooden board
three battens
hammer and horseshoe nails
lead knife
12 mm/½ in lead came
letherkin tool
barrier cream
horseshoe nails
wire (steel) wool
face mask
tallow
solder wire
soldering iron
black lead lighting putty
whiting powder
hard scrubbing brush
clean cotton rags
fire grate blackener

1 Trace the template from the back of the book, enlarging to the size required. The outer line represents the outer edge of the lead came. Mark the inner lines in felt-tipped pen. These thick lines will represent the centre of the lead came that joins the pieces of glass together.

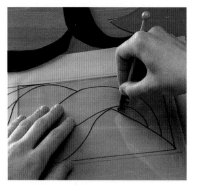

2 Lay a sheet of glass over the design and starting from one corner score along a line.

3 Using the ball end of the glass cutter, gently tap the reverse of the glass below the line you have scored. Tap until the two pieces fall apart. Use grozing pliers to nip off any small pieces of glass.

4 When all the glass pieces are cut, tape the drawing to a wooden board. Nail a batten to one side edge and the bottom edge, along the outer pencil line of the rectangle. Wearing barrier cream or rubber gloves, and using a lead knife, mark and cut pieces of lead came to fit along both edges.

5 Still wearing barrier cream or rubber gloves, and using a letherkin tool, open up the leaves of the lead. Starting at the corner, insert the pieces of glass, fitting lead came in each join.

6 Continue building up the design one piece at a time, cutting the lead and inserting the glass between the leaves of lead. Use horseshoe nails to tack and hold the lead in place as you work.

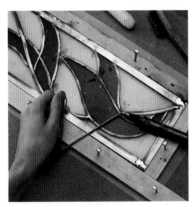

7 When the design is complete, clean the joints of lead with wire (steel) wool. Wear a mask to avoid inhaling the lead dust. Rub tallow on to each joint. Place solder wire over the joint then melt it into place with the soldering iron. When the front of the panel is finished, turn it over and repeat on the reverse.

8 Wearing barrier cream, push black lead lighting putty into the gaps between the lead came and the glass.

9 Cover the panel liberally with whiting powder. This will absorb excess oil in the putty and help it to dry more quickly. Leave the panel to harden for 1–2 hours.

10 Use a hard scrubbing brush to clean off the whiting and excess putty. Wear a face mask to prevent inhaling the toxic dust. Repeat steps 8–10 on the reverse of the panel.

11 Wearing barrier cream, coat the lead with fire grate blackener using a clean cotton rag, then polish off the excess until a deep colour is achieved.

PATTERNED BATHROOM BOTTLE

A jazzy painted bottle to brighten up your bathroom shelf. This one is decorated with a fun bubble pattern to echo the round shape of the bottle but you can experiment with your own designs to complement the shape of the bottle you pick.

YOU WILL NEED
glass bottle with a cork
felt-tipped pen
black outlining paste
glass paints in blue, green, violet and turquoise
small paintbrushes
turpentine
turquoise glass nugget
ultra-violet glue
bubble bath

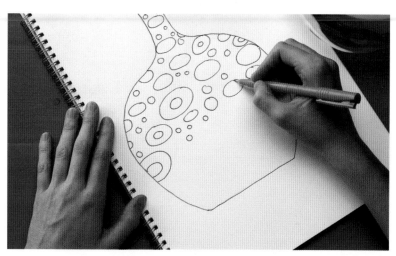

1 Decide on the pattern you would like for your bottle, then sketch your design to scale on a piece of paper.

2 Wash and thoroughly dry the bottle you have chosen. Then using a felt-tipped pen, copy your design on to the bottle.

3 Trace the design on one side of the bottle with black outlining paste. Leave to dry.

69

4 When the first side is thoroughly dry, trace the design on the other side of the bottle using outlining paste.

5 When the outlining paste is thoroughly dry, paint inside the circle motifs using blue, green and violet glass paints. Clean the paintbrushes between different colours with turpentine.

6 Once the circles are dry, paint the surrounding area using turquoise glass paint. Leave to dry.

7 Using ultra-violet glue, stick a glass nugget to the top of the cork.

8 Fill the bottle with your favourite bubble bath and replace the cork.

GLASS NUGGET WINDOW HANGING

This window hanging is an easy project that is ideal for beginners. The simple materials of muslin fabric, coloured glass and silver wire complement each other perfectly and create a pleasingly fresh, uncluttered decoration.

YOU WILL NEED
½ m/¾ yd white muslin
sharp scissors
white sewing thread
sewing needle
copyright-free pictures of shells
(see templates)
epoxy glue
four large glass nuggets
fine silver jewellery wire
jewellery pliers
thick copper wire

1 Sketch your design to scale on a piece of paper. Draw the shape of the background on to the muslin leaving extra to turn and edge the sides. Cut out the shape.

2 Sew a single hem around all the sides of the muslin rectangle.

3 Photocopy shell pictures on to acetate. Cut out the images using sharp scissors. ▶

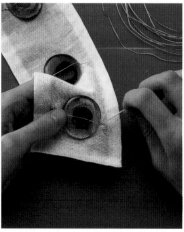

4 Glue the acetate shapes on to the muslin, spacing them equally down the muslin. Then glue the glass nuggets over the images. Make sure they do not stick to your worktop as the glue may seep through the material.

5 Cut pieces of silver wire long enough to fit across each glass nugget, leaving a little extra at either side. Curl each end into a spiral using the jewellery pliers.

6 Sew the pieces of wire securely to the muslin at each side of the glass nuggets.

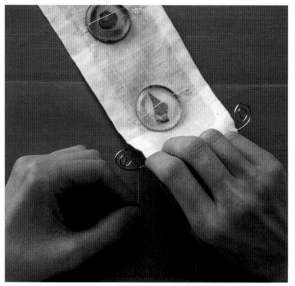

7 Take the copper wire, curl one end into a spiral using the small pliers, and slide the metal through the top hem of the material. Do the same on the bottom. Curl the other ends of both pieces of the wire when they are through.

8 Take some silver wire and wind it round the copper wire at the top end, on both sides of the material, for the piece to hang in the window.

BATHROOM CABINET DOOR PANEL

An authentic stained glass project using many glass pieces that are cut to shape to create a beautiful abstract design. This is an ambitious project, so it is best undertaken when you have had some practice working with stained glass.

YOU WILL NEED
felt-tipped pen
sheets of coloured glass
glass cutter
grozing pliers
masking tape
wooden board
three battens
hammer and horseshoe nails
lead knife
12 mm/½ in lead came
letherkin tool
barrier cream
wire (steel) brush
face mask
tallow
solder wire
soldering iron
black lead lighting putty
whiting powder
clean cotton rags
hard scrubbing brush
fire grate blackener

1 Trace the template from the back of the book, enlarging to the size required. The outer line represents the outer edge of the lead came. Go over the inner lines in felt-tipped pen. These thick lines will represent the centre of the lead came that joins the pieces of glass together.

2 Lay a sheet of glass over the design and starting from one corner score along a line.

3 Using the ball end of the glass cutter, gently tap the reverse of the glass below the line you have scored. Tap until the two pieces fall apart. Use grozing pliers to nip off any small pieces of glass.

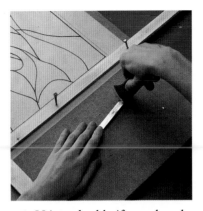

4 When all the glass is cut, tape your drawing to a board. Nail a batten to one side edge and the bottom edge, along the outer pencil line of the rectangle.

5 Using a lead knife, mark and cut a piece of lead came to fit along the side of the panel. Repeat for the bottom edge. Using a letherkin tool, open up the leaves of the lead to make it easier to insert the glass. Wear barrier cream to protect your hands from the toxic lead.

6 Build up your design one piece at a time, cutting the lead and inserting the glass between the leaves of lead. Use horseshoe nails to tack and hold the lead in place as you work.

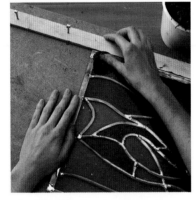

7 When the design is finished, clean the lead joints with a wire (steel) brush. Wear a mask to avoid inhaling the lead dust. Rub tallow on to each joint. Place solder wire over the joint then melt it into place with the soldering iron. When the front is finished, turn the panel over and repeat on the reverse.

8 Wearing barrier cream or rubber gloves, firmly press black lead lighting putty into the gaps between the lead came and the glass.

9 Cover the panel liberally with whiting powder. This will absorb excess oil in the putty and help it to dry more quickly. Leave the panel to harden for 1–2 hours.

▶

10 Use a hard scrubbing brush to clean off the whiting and excess putty. Wear a face mask to prevent inhaling the toxic dust. Repeat steps 8–10 on the reverse of the panel.

11 Wearing barrier cream, coat the lead with fire grate blackener using a clean cotton rag, then polish off the excess until you get a deep colour.

INDOOR GLASS LANTERN

Slip this simple four-sided lantern over a nightlight to give a colourful glow in the evenings.
This lantern is made with two plain and two panelled sections, but you could choose
four plain sides to begin with.

YOU WILL NEED
glass cutter
sheets of clear glass
sheets of stained glass in red, orange
and yellow
etching paste
rubber gloves
medium paintbrush
clean cotton rag
6 mm/¼ in copper foil
fid
flux
flux brush
solder
soldering iron
small box or block of wood
nightlight

1 Trace the templates for the indoor lantern from the back of the book, enlarging them to the size required.

2 Take a glass cutter and, using your templates as a guide, cut out two clear sides and the red, orange and yellow pieces which make up the other two sides. Cut two of each for the two sides.

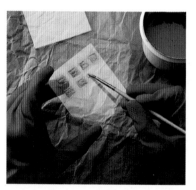

3 Using the template as a guide, take each side and paint etching paste on in squares as shown, wearing rubber gloves, for protection. Leave the paste for 3 minutes.

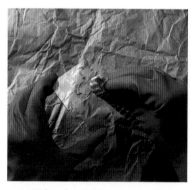

4 Take the acid etched glass to your sink and allow cold water to run freely over the glass to take the paste off. Rinse thoroughly and then dry with a clean cotton rag.

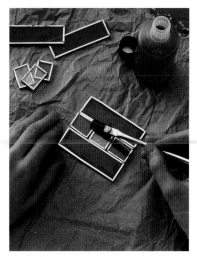

5 Wrap 6 mm/¼ in copper foil around the edges of all of the pieces of coloured and clear/etched glass.

6 Using a fid, flatten all the copper foil to smooth around the edges.

7 Place the pieces next to each other as you wish to solder them, panel by panel. Flux all the copper using a brush.

8 Tack each side together by melting a spot of solder on each joining edge. This keeps the pieces in place, and makes soldering easier.

9 Solder each side together, and then solder around the edges to complete the four panels.

▶

10 To solder the lantern together and make it three-dimensional you will need to balance the sides at a right angle on a small box or a block of wood. Flux and solder two corners so they can stand upright to make the box.

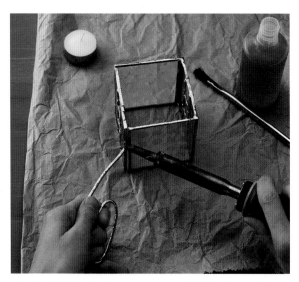

11 Solder the last two corners by fluxing and then soldering from top to bottom. Clean the glass with a clean cotton rag. Stand the nightlight on a tile and place the lantern over it. Never leave burning candles unattended and keep them away from children.

MATERIALS

A variety of materials are needed for working with stained glass including glass paints, stained glass and soldering irons, from specialist glass shops, and glass nuggets, available from craft shops.

CONTOUR PASTE
Contour paste is used to create raised lines on glass. This gives the look of leaded windows and also acts as a barrier for paints.

COPPER FOIL
This is a self-adhesive tape which is wrapped around glass so that it can be soldered together.

COPPER WIRE
Copper wire is ideal for using to make hooks and decoration. It is compatible with tin solder.

EPOXY GLUE
Epoxy glue is strong and clear and it takes a few minutes to go hard which gives you time to work.

ETCHING PASTE
Etching paste is an acid paste that eats into glass to leave a matt 'frosted' finish. Use for decorating clear and pale coloured glass.

FLUX
Flux is brushed on to copper foil to clean the metal and lower the melting point of the solder so that the solder will flow more easily.

GLASS NUGGETS
Glass nuggets are available in a wide variety of colours and sizes.

GLASS PAINTS
Glass paints are translucent and give a vibrant colour. These paints are not washable.

HORSESHOE NAILS
Horseshoe nails are used to hold glass pieces in place as you work. They are easy to remove and reduce the risk of damage to glass and lead.

MASKING TAPE
This is ideal for making straight lines for etching and painting.

SELF-ADHESIVE LEAD
Self-adhesive lead is easy to use and looks like real lead came to give an authentic stained glass window effect.

SELF-ADHESIVE VINYL
Self-adhesive vinyl is useful for masking off large areas when painting and etching the glass.

SILVER JEWELLERY WIRE
A fine wire for using as a hanging wire or decorative binding.

SOLDER
Solder is made up of tin and lead. 50 per cent tin, 50 per cent lead is the best for most projects as it flows easily.

STAINED GLASS
Stained glass is available in many colours, textures and prices.

TURPENTINE
Turpentine is used as a solvent to clean off most paints.

ULTRA-VIOLET GLUE
Ultra-violet glue goes hard in daylight. Red glass blocks ultra-violet rays, so you should let the light shine through the non-red glass when sticking two colours together, or use epoxy glue.

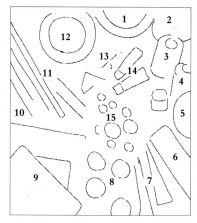

Opposite: masking tape (1), turpentine (2), solder (3), flux (4), etching paste (5), self-adhesive vinyl (6), contour paste (7), glass paints (8), stained glass (9), copper wire (10), self-adhesive lead (11), copper foil (12), horseshoe nails (13), epoxy glue (14), glass nuggets (15).

EQUIPMENT

Stained glass does require some specialist equipment, although many of the items used are commonly found in most households. The items listed below will make the job easier.

COTTON RAGS
These are needed for drying glass.

CRAFT KNIFE
This is useful for cutting lead.

EYE GOGGLES
These are vital for eye protection.

FID
A fid is used for pressing down copper foil and self-adhesive lead.

FLUX BRUSH
These inexpensive brushes are used to paint flux on copper foil.

GLASS CUTTER
A glass cutter has a wheel made of hardened metal. This is run over the glass to create a score mark, along which the glass will break.

GROZING PLIERS
Grozing pliers are used to take off any sharp shards of glass.

JEWELLERY PLIERS
These are useful for detailed work.

LEAD KNIFE
A lead knife has a curved blade to help when cutting lead came.

LEAD VICE
A lead vice is useful for stretching pieces of lead came before cutting.

LETHERKIN TOOL
This is used to open up the leaf of the lead came after you have cut it.

PAINTBRUSHES
A selection of paintbrushes are useful for applying paint and etching paste.

PLIERS
Round-nosed and square-nosed pliers are useful for straightening wire and bending sharp angles.

RUBBER GLOVES
A pair of gloves are vital to protect your hands from etching paste and toxic lead.

RULER
A ruler is essential for measuring.

SCISSORS
A pair of small, sharp scissors are useful for many cutting tasks.

SCYTHE STONE
A scythe stone removes the sharp edges left after glass has been cut. Use this tool on every piece of glass you cut.

SOLDERING IRON
You will need a 75-watt (or higher) soldering iron. You will need a stand for the hot iron.

SPONGES
Sponges cut into pieces are ideal for applying paint over a large area of glass.

TALLOW STICK
Tallow is the traditional alternative to liquid soldering flux.

WIRE CUTTERS
These can cut wire neatly.

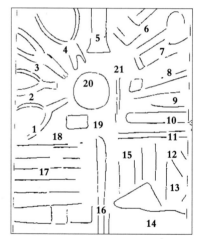

Opposite: jewellery pliers (1), round-nosed pliers (2), grozing pliers (3), square-nosed pliers (4), lead knife (5), lead vice (6), scissors (7), letherkin tool (8), craft knife (9), wooden fid (10), tallow stick (11), soldering iron (12), rubber gloves (13), cotton rags (14), rulers (15), wire (steel) brush (16) paintbrushes (17), flux brush (18), sponge (19), wire (steel) wool (20), glass cutter (21).

TECHNIQUES

On the following pages you will find useful step-by-step descriptions of some of the basic techniques, which will help you to perfect your skills and achieve beautiful and successful results.

ETCHING GLASS

1 Self-adhesive vinyl makes a good mask when etching. Cut out shapes from self-adhesive vinyl. Decide where you want to position them on the glass, remove the backing paper and stick down.

2 Wearing rubber gloves, paint the etching paste evenly over the vase with a paintbrush, make sure you do not spread it too thinly, or you will find the effect quite faint. Leave to dry for 3 minutes.

3 Still wearing the rubber gloves, wash the paste off under a running tap. Then wipe off any residue and rinse. Peel off the shapes, wash again. Dry the glass with a clean cotton rag.

PAINTING GLASS

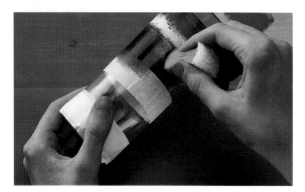 

1 Glass paints should be used with turpentine. Use masking tape for large areas to define the edges. Pour a small drop of paint on to a tile or saucer, take a small piece of sponge and dab it into the paint and then on to the glass.

2 Take a small paintbrush and paint freestyle on to the glass. Remember to clean your brush immediately you have finished with one colour so that it does not go hard.

CUTTING GLASS

1 Hold the cutter with your index finger on top of the cutter, and your thumb and second finger gripping each side, with the grozing teeth facing towards your elbow. This may seem awkward at first, but when you are cutting correctly with the cutter at right angles to the glass, this position will give you lots of movement in your arm.

2 Always cut the glass from edge to edge, one cut at a time. So start, as shown here, at one edge with your cutter at right angles to the glass. Make a consistent cut from one edge to the other.

3 Now you can break the glass where you have made your score mark. The first way is to hold your cutter upside down between your thumb and first finger. Hold it loosely so that you can swing it to hit the underside of the score mark with the ball on the end of the cutter. Tap along the score mark following the crack along. The glass will just break off.

4 The second way is to hold the glass with your hands both sides of the score mark at one end. Apply firm pressure pulling down and away from the crack. This method is only good for very straight score marks.

5 The last method of breaking your score line is to put the cutter on the table and place the glass on the cutter with the score mark over the cutter.

6 With the base of your thumbs put pressure on both sides of the score mark. Push down until the glass breaks.

FOILING GLASS

  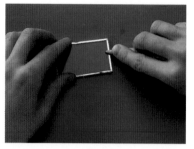

1 Hold the foil between your fingers, as shown, and use your thumb to peel back the protective backing paper as you work around the glass. Try not to touch the adhesive side of the tape as it will not stick properly if it is greasy or dusty.

2 Stick the foil to the edge of the glass, all the way around, and overlap the end by 1 cm/½ in.

3 Using two fingertips, press the foil down on to both sides of the glass, all the way around. Now use the fid to flatten the foil on to the glass to ensure it is stuck firmly all the way around.

SOLDERING GLASS

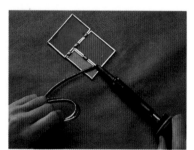  

1 Using a flux brush, apply the flux to all the copper foil showing on the first side. Take the soldering iron so the tip of the iron side faces side to side and the thin side faces up and down. Hold the solder in the other hand with 10 cm/4 in uncoiled. Tack the pieces together by melting a blob of solder on to each joining edge. This keeps the pieces in place while you solder them together.

2 Melt the solder, and allow it to run along the copper. Do not let it go too flat, but make sure you have a small drop of solder. This makes it look neater and, more importantly, is stronger. Turn the piece over, flux and solder the other side.

3 Tin the edges by firstly fluxing, and then running the soldering iron along the edge. There is usually enough solder on the edge to spread around.

USING LEAD CAME

Lead came usually comes in 2 m/
2¼ yd lengths. If you look at the
end of a piece of lead came you
will see that it is shaped like an
'H'. The central bar of the came is
known as the heart or core. The
flat strips at the top and bottom of
the heart are known as the leaf.
The heart of the came keeps the
two pieces of glass apart when you
put a panel together. The leaf will
stop the glass from falling out of
the panel when it is finished.

1 When drawing out your
design, mark the outline of
each piece of glass. This outline
represents the heart of the lead. A
medium-width felt-tipped pen is
best as the mark is the same width
as the lead. It is important when
cutting glass for your panel that
you cut each separate piece on the
inside of the outline of each piece.

2 Lead came is a very pliable
material and will need to be
gently stretched to remove any
kinks or twists, therefore making
it easier to shape and cut.
To stretch lead came, you will
need a spring-loaded lead vice.
Secure the vice to a bench and
place one end of the came in
the vice. Then, using a pair of
flat-nosed pliers, grip the other
end and pull. If the vice is
spring-loaded it will automatically
grip the other end as you do so.
Take care: lead, especially thin
lead, stretches very quickly and
will break easily.

3 Using a lead knife, first bend the came to the
shape of the edge of the piece of glass. Using the
blade of the knife, mark across the leaf where you will
be cutting (remember to leave it a little short to
accommodate the leaf of the piece crossing it). Lay the
piece of came leaf down on a flat surface. Place the
knife in position and push down in a gentle but firm
rocking motion until you are right through the came.
Try to cut directly down and not at an angle, to
ensure that you will not get any awkward gaps.

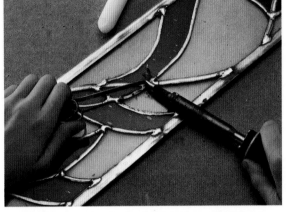

4 Soldering wire for leaded panels contains lead, so
wear barrier cream to protect your hands.
Holding the soldering wire in your left hand, lower
the tip of the soldering iron for a few seconds to melt
the solder and join the lead came.

TEMPLATES

Enlarge the templates on a photocopier, or trace the design and draw a grid of evenly spaced

squares over your tracing. Draw a larger grid on to another piece of paper and copy the

outline square by square. Draw over the lines to make sure they are continuous.

*Curtain
Decorations
pp 14–17
and
Glass Nugget Window Hanging
pp 71–3.
Same size.*

*Sun Light Catcher
pp 31–3.
Scale up.*

Door Number Plaque
pp 34–7.
Scale up.

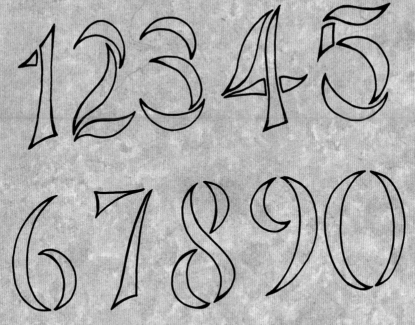

Trinket Box
pp 44–7.
Scale up.

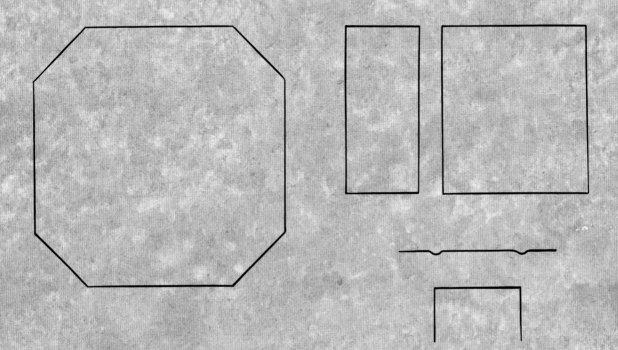

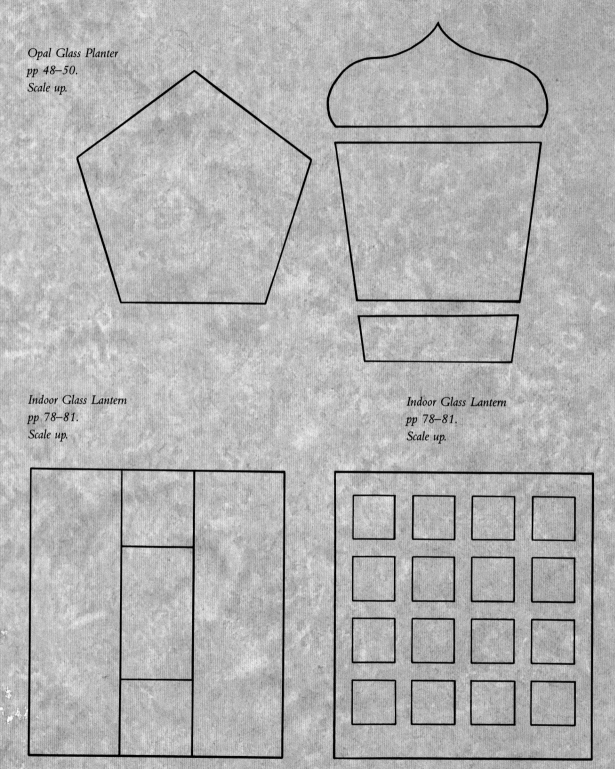

Opal Glass Planter
pp 48–50.
Scale up.

Indoor Glass Lantern
pp 78–81.
Scale up.

Indoor Glass Lantern
pp 78–81.
Scale up.

*Kitchen
Cabinet
Door Panel
pp 64–7.
Scale up.*

*Bathroom
Cabinet
Door Panel
pp 74–7
Scale up.*

SUPPLIERS

The specialist materials and equipment that you will require for the projects are available from the stores listed below.

UNITED KINGDOM

Lead and Light
35A Hartland Road
Camden Town
London NW1 8DB
Tel: (0171) 485 0997
Suppliers of soldering and glass-cutting equipment, etching paste, stained glass, copper foil and glass paints

**North Western Lead
 Company Ltd**
Newton Moor Industrial Estate
Mill Street
Hyde
Cheshire SK14 4LJ
Tel: (0161) 368 4491
Suppliers of self-adhesive lead

Codu Glassworks
43 Union Street
Maidstone
Kent ME14 1ED
Tel: (01622) 763615
Suppliers of self-adhesive lead

Kernowcraft
Freepost
Bolingey
Perranporth
Cornwall TR6 0DH
Tel: (01872) 573888
Suppliers of jeweller's round-nosed and straight-nosed pliers and fine wire-cutters

Philip & Tacey Ltd
Tel: (01264) 332171
Pébéo Vitrail glass paints and contour paste are available from selected art and craft shops – call Philip & Tacey for details of your nearest stockist

AUSTRALIA

Pébéo Australia
Tel: (613) 9416 0611
Call for details of your nearest stockist

The Stained Glass Centre
221 Hale Street
Peterie Terrace
Queensland 4000

Lincraft
Tel: (03) 9875 7575
Stores in every capital city except Darwin – call for details of your nearest store

CANADA

Pébéo Canada
Tel: (819) 829 5012
Call for details of your nearest stockist

ACKNOWLEDGEMENTS

The publishers would like to thank the following people for designing the projects in this book: Michael Ball for the Banded Vase pp 8-10, Door Number Plaque pp 34-37, Opal Glass Planter pp 48-50; Anna-Lise De'Ath for the Mosaic Lantern pp 11-13, Leaded Picture Frames pp 18-20, Leaded Door Panels pp 28-30, Sun Light Catcher pp 31-33, Patterned Bathroom Bottle pp 68-71; Emma Micklethwaite for the Kitchen Cabinet Door Panel pp 64-67, Bathroom Cabinet Door Panel pp 74-77; Deidre O'Malley for the Curtain Decorations pp 14-17, Diamond Patterned Carafe pp 21-23, Etched Bathroom Mirror pp 41-43, Mosaic-Banded Candle Holder pp 51-53, Glass Nugget Window Hanging pp 71-73, Indoor Glass Lantern pp 78-81; Polly Plouviez for the Fringed Candlestick pp 24-27, Glass Nugget Bottle Holder pp 38-40, Glass Nugget Wall Clock pp 54-57, Kitchen Storage Jar pp 58-60, Painted Salt & Pepper Pots pp 61-63.

INDEX